AN EERIE ADULT COLOURING BOOK

HORRORSCOPE

Illustrated

by

Sarah Pain

CLAN DESTINE COLOURING ADVENTURES

First published in Australia 2016
by Clan Destine Press
　PO Box 121 Bittern
　Victoria 3918 Australia

Copyright © Sarah Pain

All rights reserved. No part of this book may be reproduced or transmitted in any form or by any means, electronic or mechanical, including photocopying, recording or by any information storage and retrieval system, without prior permission in writing from the publisher. The *Australian Copyright Act 1968* (The Act) allows a maximum of one chapter or 10 per cent of any book, whichever is the greater, to be photocopied by any educational institution for its educational purposes provided that the educational institution (or the body that administers it) has given a remuneration notice to Copyright Agency Limited (CAL) under the Act.

National Library of Australia Cataloguing-in-Publication entry

Ilustrator:　Pain, Sarah

Title:　Horrorscope
　　　　　Eerie Adult Colouring Book

ISBN　(pbk) 978-0-9943538-9-4

Cover Design:　Sarah Pain

Illustrations:　Sarah Pain

Design & Typesetting: Clan Destine Press

Printed and bound in Australia by Lightning Source

　　　　　www.clandestinepress.com.au

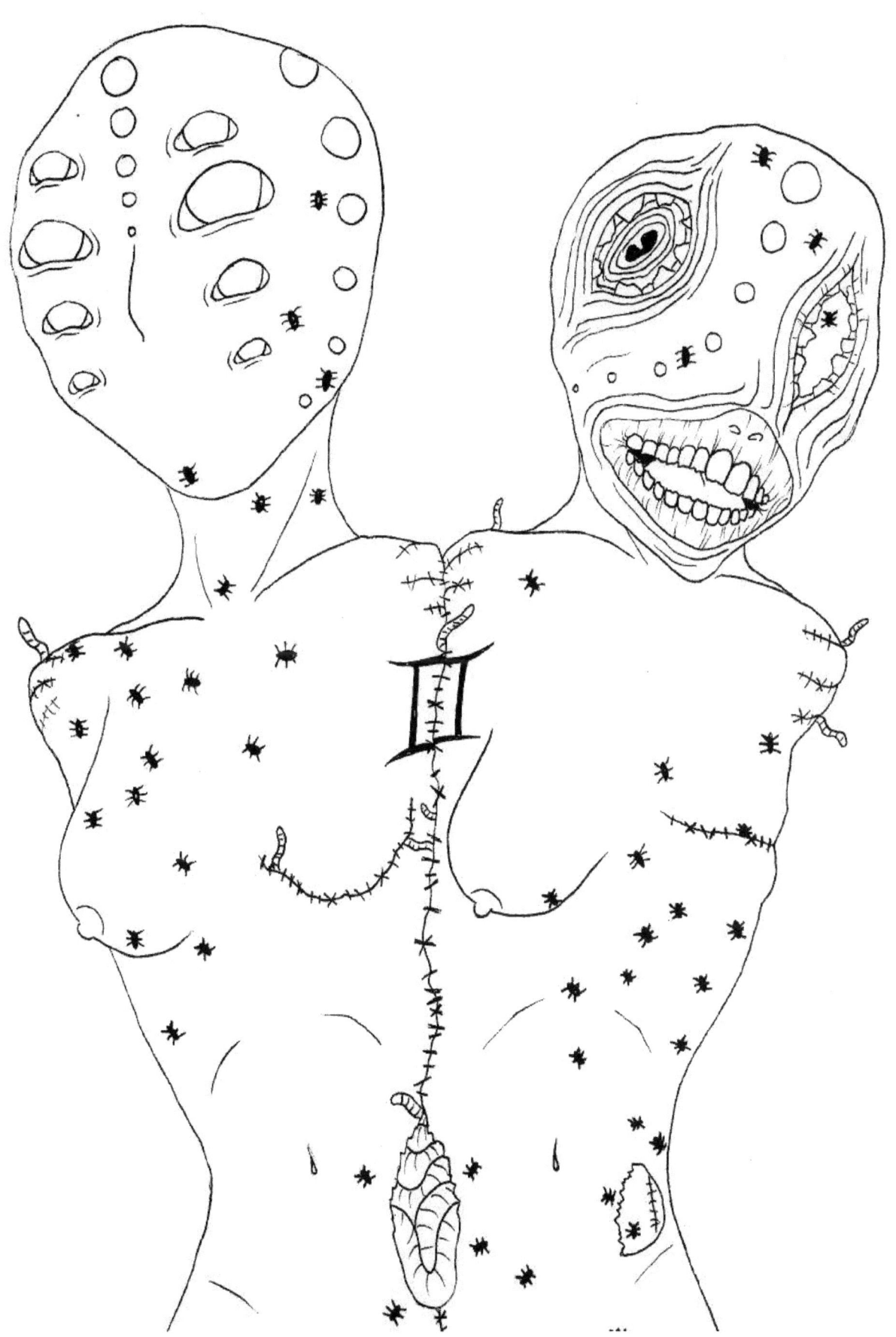

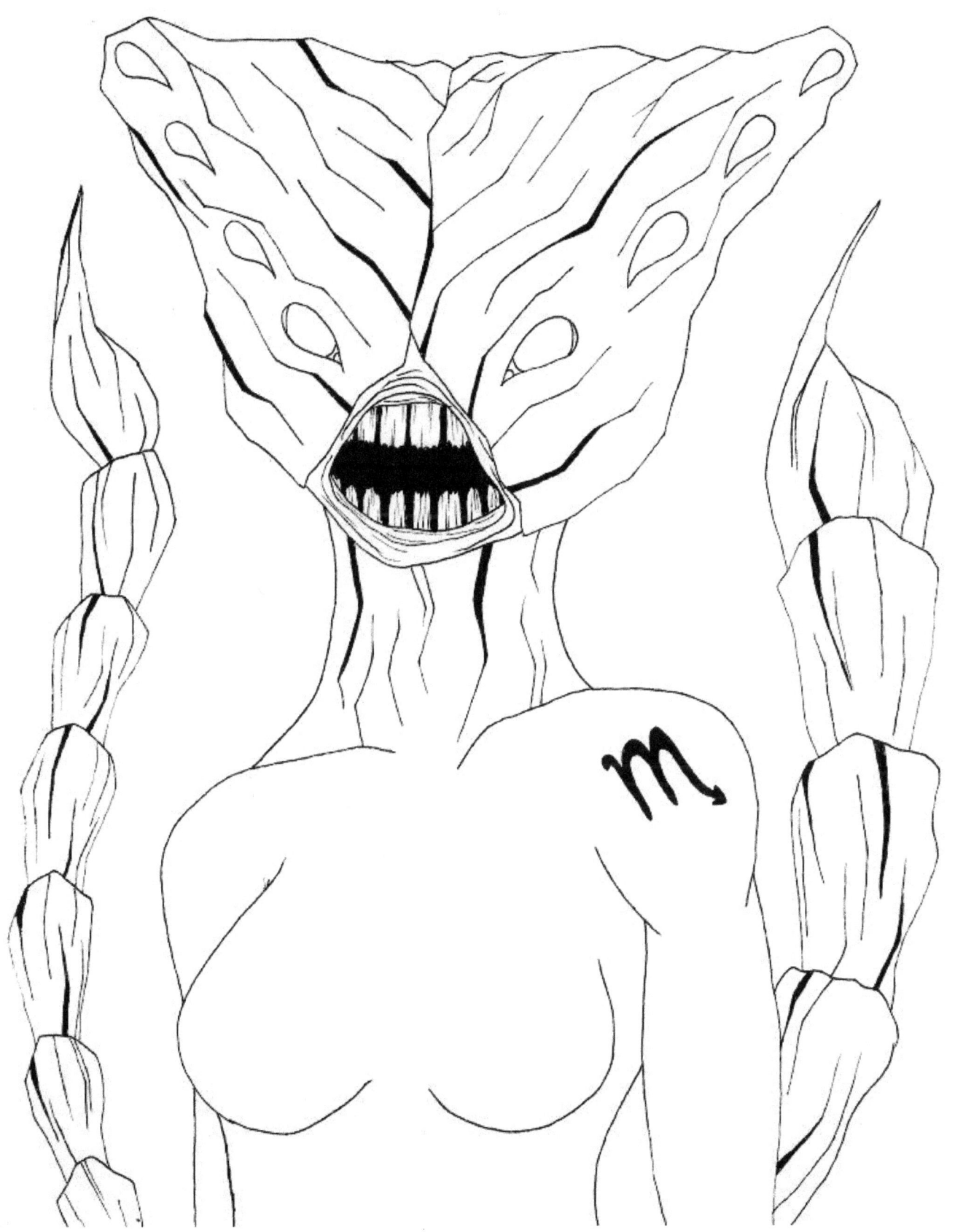

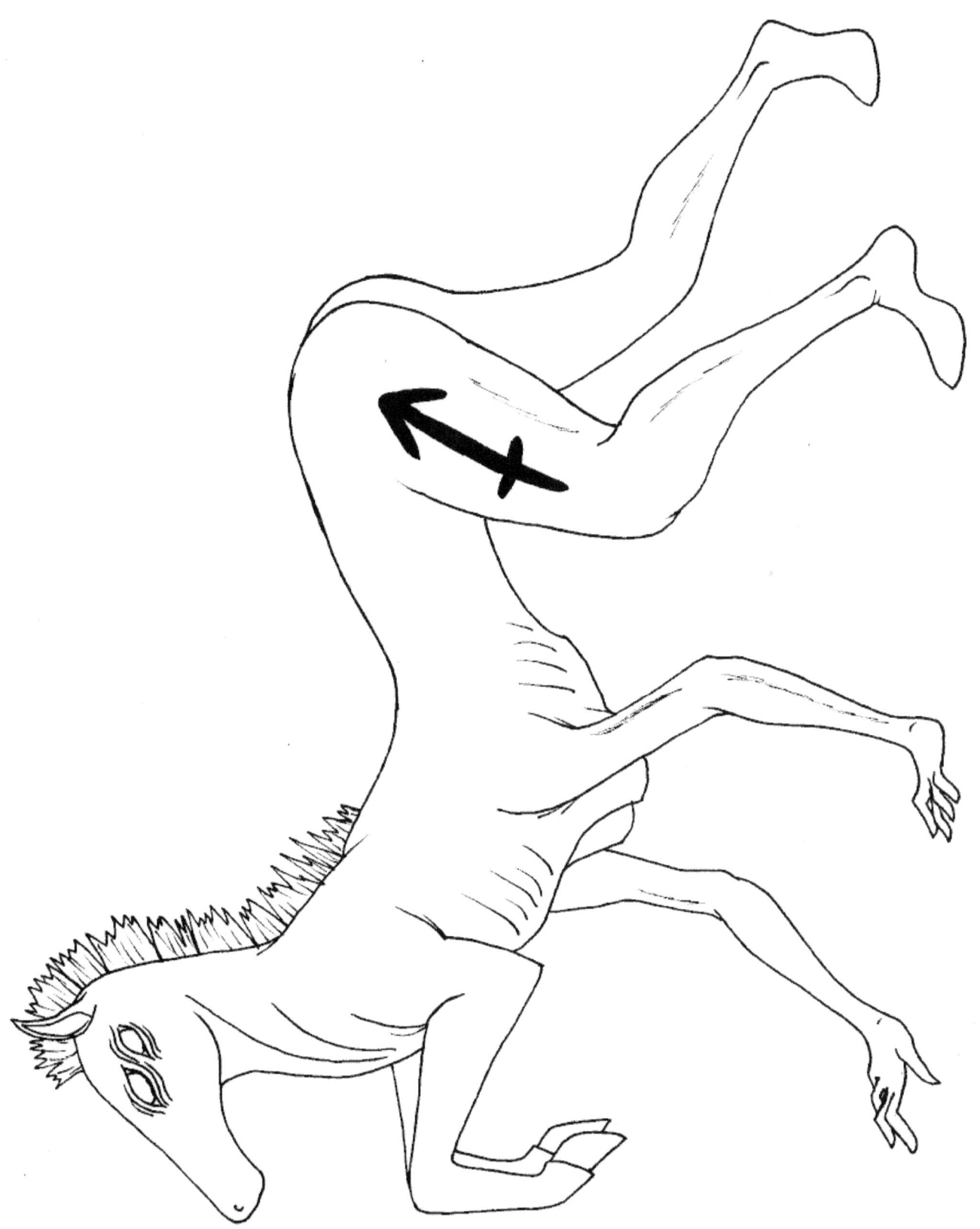

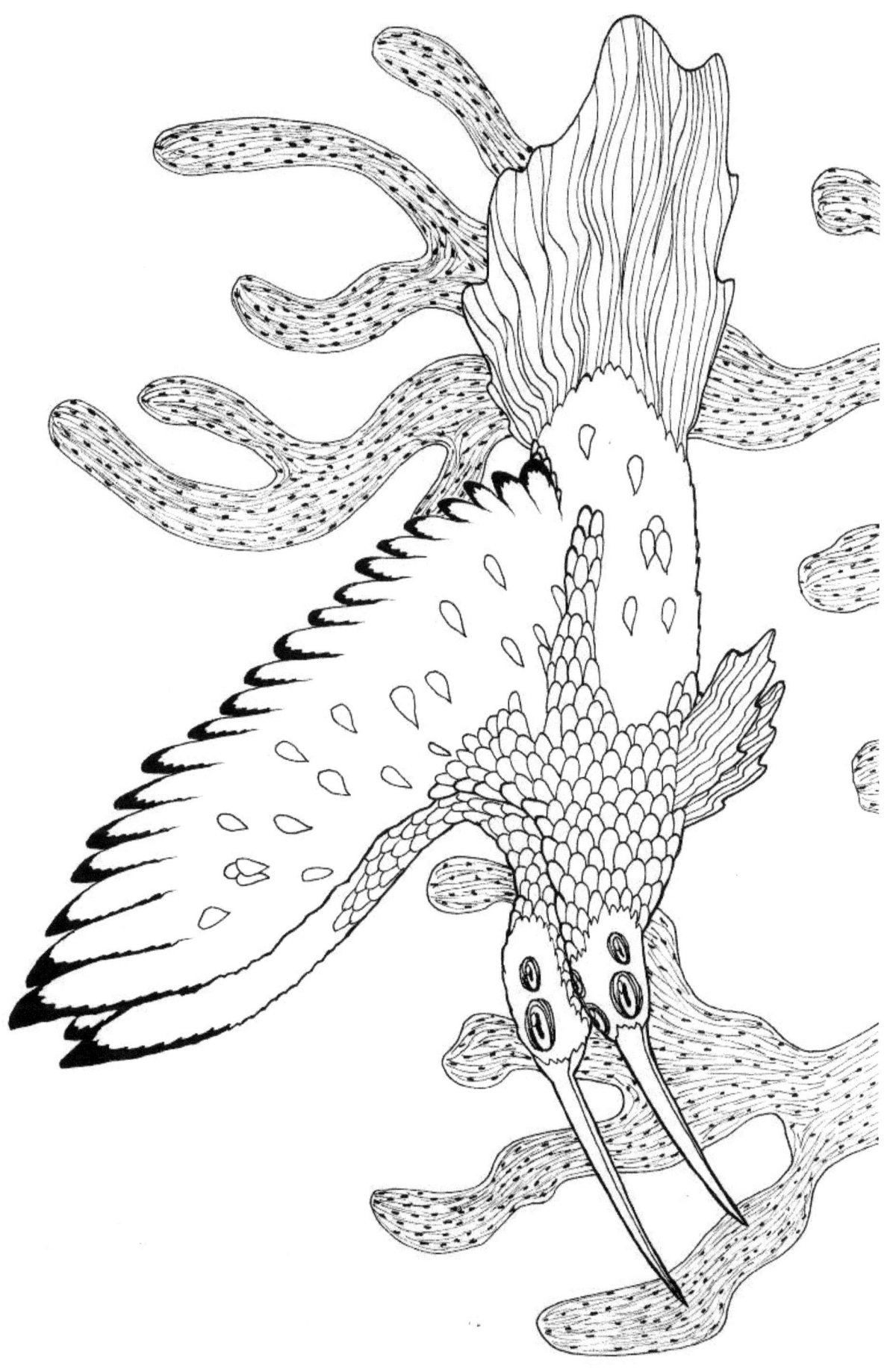

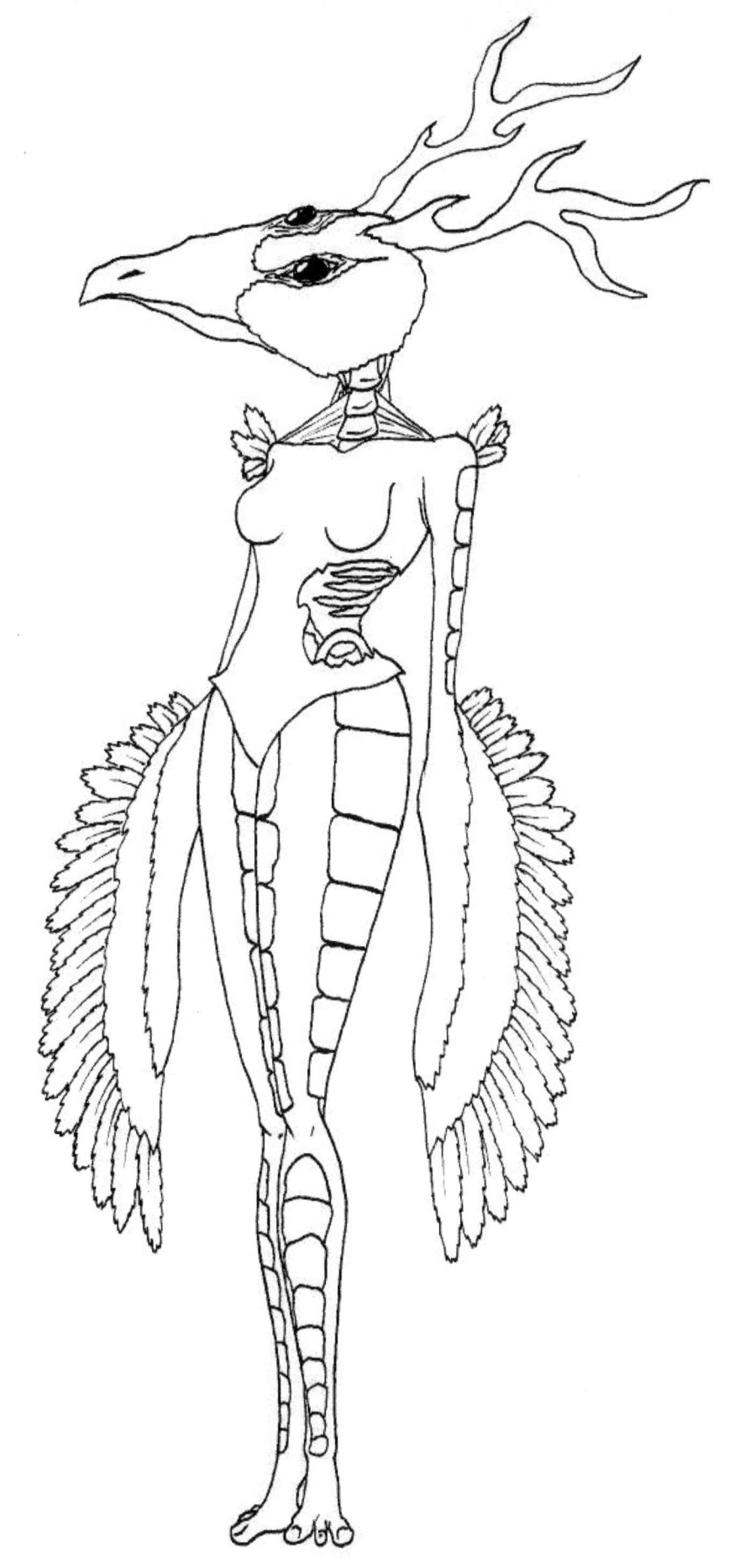

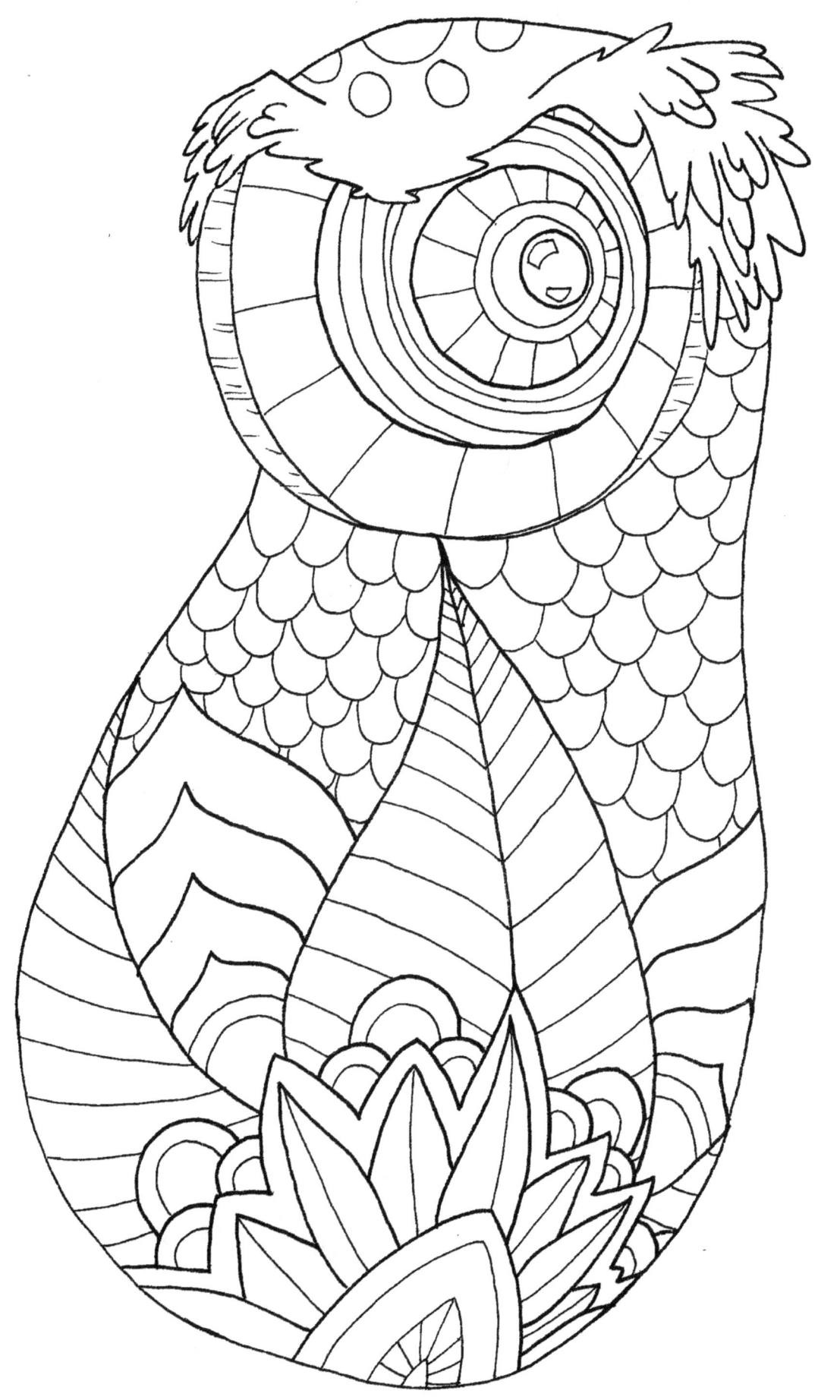

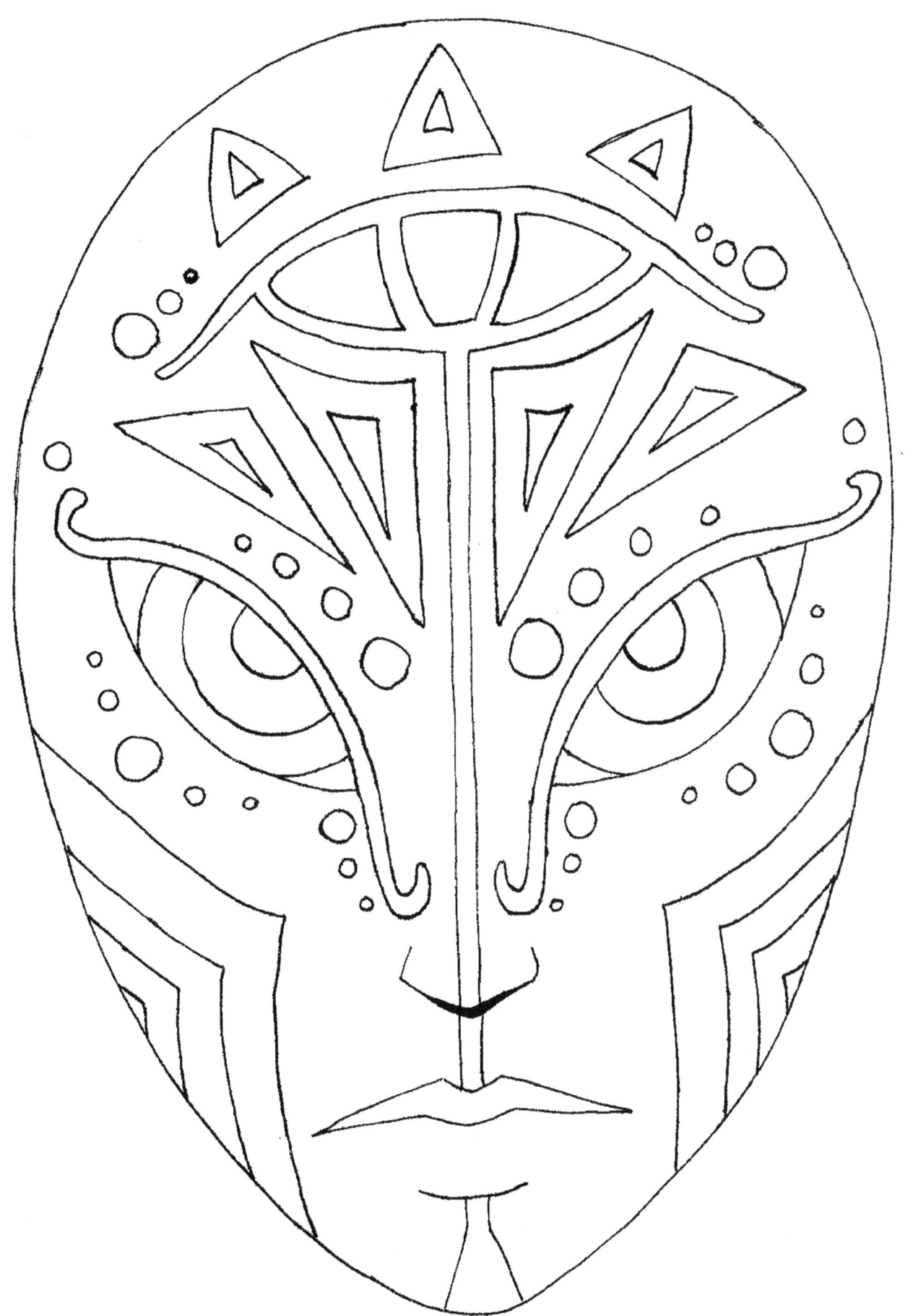

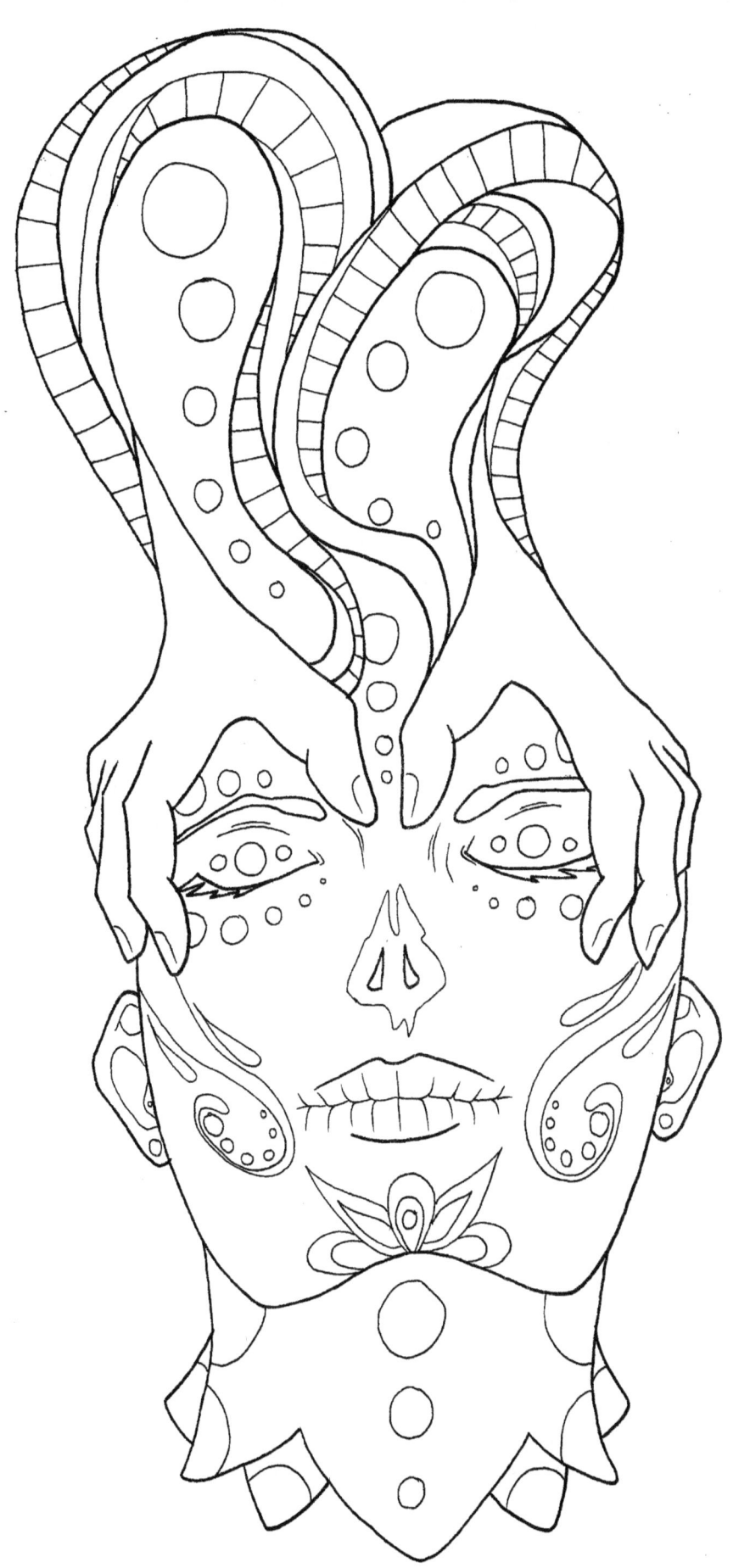

Also from

CLAN DESTINE PRESS

The Colouring Bazaar

Illustrated by

Ashlea Bechaz

The Journal of Infinite Possibility

Illustrated by

Ashlea Bechaz, Sarah Pain,
Vicky Pratt & Loraine Cooper

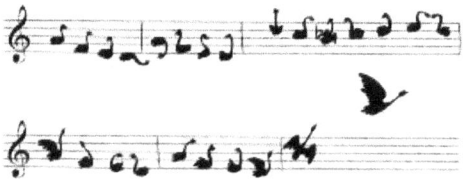

www.ingramcontent.com/pod-product-compliance
Lightning Source LLC
LaVergne TN
LVHW061303060426
835510LV00014B/1854